DEVELOP SELF-REGULATION SKILLS

Workbook For Kids

CBT Activities To help Children Overcome Strong Emotions, Become Confident, And Exceed Expectations At School

Sibley Hall

About the Author

The author is trained in cognitive behavioral therapy. She has been using it in her clinical practice for six years now. Sibley has completed three courses on cognitive behavioral therapy. The courses were on CBT for depression, anxiety, and personality disorders.

The author works in a private psychiatric clinic where she gives psychological and rehabilitation services. She "cognitively" conceptualizes clients and attempts to manage them through the techniques and strategies of cognitive behavioral therapy. The clients come from different age groups, with diverse sociocultural backgrounds and locations, and suffer from different emotional and behavioral deviances with varying severity levels. Mood and anxiety disorders, substance-use disorders, and non-medical problems like psychogenic pain, anger outbursts, and chronic sadness are some of the most common cases.

The author also integrates cognitive behavioral therapy with eclectic therapy. Eclectic therapy is a flexible and multifaceted approach to therapy that aids a clinician in understanding and managing clients as per their unique needs and preferences. This approach has a clinical significance as it equips the clients to express themselves and adaptively cope with the challenges and complexities of the modern world.

TABLE OF CONTENTS

DEAR NURTURERS

Do you think you are raising a difficult child?

Have you diagnosed the "difficulty" element in your child, or are you in the process of figuring it out? Unfortunately, things are really "difficult" and "complicated" when you are dealing with the superior most and a continuously evolving creature – the human; why? Because this creature carries a unique and magnificently designed brain that is enclosed in a skull. What really happens in the brain, both at the hardware and software levels, is difficult to identify, understand and predict. Today, all parents want happy, calm, and well-behaved children. This is a goal for some parents, but passion and "craze" for other parents. Parents normally try to satisfy themselves and achieve this goal through empathy, social skills and play that they incorporate into their child-rearing practices. In reality, things are different, and they really are. The brain is like a universe that goes through significant changes from breastfeeding to disciple to education. So, your child undergoes a lot of psychological changes as a result of diverse multiple inputs and stimulation from their environment.

Activities found in this book can help you and your child to identify and understand their problems, and, above all, you will discover the "what" and "who" - What are your child's problems? And who is responsible for those problems? All is explained. The activities are based on the strategies of Cognitive Behavioral Therapy (CBT). Cognitive behavioral therapy is a scientifically proven therapeutic intervention that focuses on psychosocial determinants and how they influence thoughts and perceptions, responses, and behaviors. This book addresses a wide range of psychological problems: mood problems, behavioral issues, changes in appetite, and quality of life issues. This book will teach your child a set of skills to actively take control of himself/ herself so that he/ she may live a happier and healthier life. Although this book is for children, you, as nurturers, will be playing a crucial part in helping your child take control over their emotional states, identifying the root cause of their problems, and making them their own "masters."Of course, things will not be that straightforward as you have to stick close to your child and help them with the activities throughout this book.

Please remember that the guidelines and skills in this book are based on scientific models. They are valid and reliable, with excellent generalizability across different regions and cultures. If you make your child follow and practice, you will see the results. Parenting is difficult, and it becomes even more difficult when a parent is not able to understand changes and deviances in their child, but your commitment and dedication to the techniques explained in this book are everything you and your child need to succeed.

A WORD FOR CHILDREN

This book goes to you!

Do you ever feel like unwanted and unpleasant emotions are taking control over you and your life as a whole? Do you feel like your life is not under your control, and somebody else is controlling your life? Do you experience anything like chronic sleeplessness, irritability, fear or anxiety, boredom, and aggression on minor issues and without any medical reason? All such feelings and states can create multiple problems at home, school, and other situations. These will collectively turn on your "UNFUN" button, and you will withdraw from situations and activities which were once bringing fun into your life – like spending time with family or friends, playing, watching television, going on a holiday/ vacation, and even birthdays. The state or the situation can be a lot worse when problems and emotional states become hard to explain, especially to immediate family members. Well, the truth is not bitter. All these unwanted and uncomfortable emotions and feelings can be controlled. This book will show you how you can really be your own boss and how you can prevent and manage your problems by yourself at the right time and at the right place.

INTRODUCTION

Have you ever wondered what is happening in this globe?

There is an epidemic of stress that is causing a growing problem with people's happiness levels across the planet. Countless articles, studies, and news reports today tell us about psychiatric medication, particularly antidepressants, whose consumption surged from 2010 to 2022. The matter is not about adults and/ or elderly people. Current statistics show that millions of children are being diagnosed with, are prescribed psychiatric medication, and are enrolled in sessions for counseling and/ or psychotherapy for a number of emotional-behavioral problems; emotional dysregulation, low frustration tolerance, and low self-esteem. Children are being clinically diagnosed with some psychological disorder(s) too. Today, millions of children worldwide are taking Ritalin, a central nervous system stimulant medication used to manage attention deficit hyperactivity disorder.

Have you ever thought about all of this?

Why are the global statistics related to children's psychological problems getting higher day by day?

Why are children fighting with obesity and the early onset of puberty? Current mental health professionals call this "precocious puberty."

It is unfortunate to see that most of us don't even question this as strange; it's just the way things are. People prefer staying comfortable. "My son is on psychiatric medication," "My daughter is taking Prozac," or "My child is shy, but things should get better with time." How can things proceed like this? How do parents utter all this nonchalantly? Why are stress levels of children high today because of excessive fear and anxiety of being judged and evaluated by parents, significant elders, teachers, and others? Are "Parental norms" or "societal norms" flawed, or is there something else?

This is a book about Cognitive Behavioral Therapy (CBT) for children. Cognitive behavioral therapy helps to discover the "glasses" – What if you were to discover that the glasses you are wearing are carrying a wrong prescription about the self, others, and the world? What if you were not able to see things as clearly as you thought? How about changing the lenses, correcting vision, and looking again at the world? Behold, you will find the ways and mechanisms in this book to look different. You will learn to see things from a different and new perspective, with new lenses, and eventually with real and constructive binoculars of your own. You will be examining your "default settings," inputs from multiple situations and environments through different activities and play. Activities and play have been added to this book because it is not a relief from serious learning. For you as a child, activities, and play are a means of "serious" learning. Therefore, you will be solving the riddles of "the self" and the world that can be highly painful when remained unresolved.

A Quick Glance at Cognitive-Behavioral Therapy (CBT)

Cognitive Behavioral Therapy (CBT) was invented by the late but great mental health professional Aaron T. Beck in the 1960s. Beck's contribution to the field of mental health is highly appreciable, and he holds a place under the umbrella of "one of the five most influential psychotherapists of all time." In his lifetime, he authored/ co-authored 25 books and published over 600 scientific articles.

Aaron T. Beck used to practice as a psychoanalyst. A psychotherapist who was trained and who used to assess and manage psychological problems through psychoanalysis was known as a psychoanalyst. Psychoanalysis was very popular during the 1950s as it was the only dominant perspective of psychology. A psychoanalyst used to conduct very detailed, very long, time-consuming sessions with clients, where his/her early childhood memories, trauma, early and/ or delayed gratification of the needs, and the fixations during childhood were assessed. It was firmly believed that all of these were significant contributors to the psychological and emotional problems of mankind that were expressed later in life.

Psychoanalysis, as a spine of psychology and psychotherapy, was like a religion to everybody, from laypeople to trained mental health professionals. It was a mutual consensus that early childhood memories had a significant impact in later life as they became "part of you" like a shadow. You may not be aware of these memories as they are the part of your "unconscious" that is affecting you directly or indirectly, and as a result, you experience a lot of emotions like sadness, joy, anxiety, and gratitude. Similarly, you respond differently in different situations. You show tantrums, anger, fear, a state of calmness, etc. Sometimes you can gain control over yourself, while at other times, things are beyond your reach. It was concluded by the psychoanalysts that all this was the expression, the impact of the "unconscious" that has its roots in early childhood.

Like everybody else in the 1950s, Aaron T. Beck was mesmerized by psychoanalysis and the "unconscious" side of the mind. A trained professional from Providence, Rhode Island, wanted to empirically convince his pupils about psychoanalysis. He wanted to explore and validate psychoanalysis through research. To meet this purpose, Beck started to deal with adult clients, specifically those who were suffering from depression. He wanted to explore their "unconscious" by investigating their early childhood memories, especially "repressed childhood memories," as Beck, as a psychoanalyst, believed such memories are buried alive in the unconscious, which can be a prime contributor to the development of psychological problems like chronic sadness and depression. To explore this, he used classic psychoanalytical methods like free association and catharsis. In free association and catharsis, a client is freely allowed to speak and express themself without any resistance, and it is the sole responsibility of the psychoanalyst to remove the barriers and the resistance that comes in the way of this emotional expression or the other way around, this "unconscious" display.

After multiple therapy sessions with multiple people, A light in Beck's head illuminated. He was not able to empirically validate psychoanalysis and the typical psychoanalytical methods, particularly in the management of depression. Instead of scientifically validating psychoanalysis, Beck began to oppose the effectiveness of psychoanalysis. He started to question the effectiveness of psychoanalysis and the unconscious forces, specifically in the treatment of depression. All of this happened due to an accidental discovery.

Beck discovered that people that were approaching him for the treatment of depression had negative automatic thoughts that were related to their self, others, and the world. Classic psychoanalytical theories claim depression is developed as a result of unresolved hostile forces that one directs to himself. It becomes an innate need to suffer. Beck not only opposed this paradigmatic conclusion of the 1950s but empirically challenged it. Beck's interest, enthusiasm, and efforts paid off as the very first work, "Thinking and Depression: Idiosyncratic Content and Cognitive Distortions," was published in 1963. Presently, it is acknowledged as the first publication on Cognitive Behavior Therapy (CBT).

Beck's work was exemplary because he came up with a unique approach. Instead of long and time-consuming sessions that solely focused on early childhood memories and unconscious factors, he aimed at unrealistic automatic thoughts, and by adopting a collaborative role, he helped clients to test the authenticity and usefulness of the thoughts that were popping up in their minds and which are beyond their voluntary control. He also helped them to modify and change the ways by which they see and evaluate situations, themselves, and others. This "change" changes the whole string of emotions and other reactions. All of this is discussed in detail in the subsequent contents of the book. Today, Cognitive Behavioral Therapy (CBT) is considered a time-sensitive, structured, and present-oriented psychotherapy that aims to look at your thinking and the beliefs which you hold (you will find this in detail in the later chapters).

Currently, Cognitive Behavioral Therapy is quite popular throughout the globe. It originated in Europe (United States), and now it can be seen across Africa, Australia, The Middle East, and Asia. A bulk of scientific articles have been published, and a lot of books, materials, and guides are printed on the usefulness (effectiveness) of CBT in different languages. After a mutual consensus, worldwide mental health professionals have declared CBT as an ever-green, time-sensitive, structured, and the most constructive psychotherapy.

Cognitive Behavioral Therapy can help you with depression, anxiety, different medical conditions, trauma-related problems, eating problems like weight gain and obesity, and quality of life issues such as sleep difficulties, problems in relationships, stress, and anger.

Why is cognitive behavioral therapy the most effective psychotherapy?

Activity Time (1.1)

- Ivy says, "If I attempt this test, I might freeze and fail."

- Oliver says, "I must shout at others to make things right."

- Archie says, "I deserve to be sad because my soccer team lost twice."

- Rosie says, "All girls are sweet."

- Olivia says, "All boys are mischievous."

- Who is right and/or wrong among these five?
- Explain the reason behind your selection.
- What suggestions will you give to the one who you marked as "wrong"?

Please fill out the following worksheet;

Names	Mark Right or Wrong ✓ ✗	Reasons/ Suggestions
Ivy		
Oliver		
Archie		
Rosie		
Olivia		

In conclusion, this is Cognitive Behavioral Therapy (CBT). It looks at the ways of thinking. It has a belief that is; "Thinking makes feelings and behaviors." It emphasizes on the fact; "The way we think is the way we feel." You will definitely be learning more about this in the subsequent chapters of this book.

Carefully go through the following and fill out the worksheet at the end:

☘ Mickey  thinks of a chocolate  and feels happiness 

☘ Gumball  thinks to live with his siblings  and feels wonderful 

☘ Emma  thinks that she cannot perform well in sports  and feels sad about it 

 William  thinks that he will definitely fail

in his exams  therefore he feels

anxious about them 

S. No.	I THINK.....	THEREFORE I FEEL.....
1.		
2.		
3.		
4.		
5.		

Special Bonus!

Want this bonus book for FREE?

Get FREE access to it and all of my upcoming books by joining the fan base.

Scan W/ Your Camera To Join!

Chapter 2

We Demand CBT Together

In order to fully understand and apply techniques of Cognitive Behavioral Therapy (CBT) in our daily life we need to understand a few concepts. At first, we need to understand the cognitive perspective. This is a perspective in psychology that is concerned with understanding the mental processes that we humans have. These mental processes cannot be observed, they are within us and are covert in nature such as memory, perception, thinking and problem-solving. Cognitive perspective also focuses on the impact of the mental processes on behavior. It holds a strong view which states that humans are the "thinking" organisms and/ or they are the "thinkers" who construe a situation in a diverse way, distinct from each other, and react accordingly. To sum up, cognitive perspective explains individual differences in behavior with respect to differences in the way people think and process information.

Examples:

1. Zoey loves to watch The Adventures of Paddington Bear whereas Aria loves to watch The Adventures of Tintin.

2. Mila gets happy after playing tennis whereas Sophia gets happy after playing badminton.

3. Jack is fond of writing comics and reading different novels. On the other hand, his younger brother Nathan is fond of making different kinds of sculptures.

Apparently, we humans look alike but we are completely different from one another. In the current era, mental health professionals explain it through the "bio-psychosocial model" which states that all humans are different from each other, both, biologically and psychosocially.

In order to develop a better understanding of bio-psychosocial elements, kindly go through the following table with a parent. Please fill out the remainder biological factors with a parent.

Biological Factors	Psychosocial Factors
Genetic influences/ vulnerabilities	Family
Gender	Family relationships
Temperament	School (education)
Physical health	Peers
Birth order	Neighbors
	Coping skills
	Social skills
	Self-esteem
	Influence of mass media

So by keeping in view the aforementioned bio-psychosocial elements it can be concluded that all humans are different from each other and you can now better understand why Zoey, Aria, Mila, Sophia, Jack and Nathan hold different interests from each other.

? How do you see yourself?

? Are you like others?

? Are you different from others?

Please fill out the following worksheet;

S. No.	Which bio-psychosocial elements make you like others?	Which bio-psychosocial elements make you different from others?
1.		
2.		
3.		
4.		
5.		

After the cognitive perspective and bio-psychosocial model, let's learn the S-R paradigm. Our mental processes involve stimulus-response (S-R) paradigm. Stimulus could be any internal or external factor that can evoke response in an organism. Internal stimuli are those factors which arise from inside the body whereas external stimuli are those factors which come from the surroundings (external environment) and are detected by the senses. Human-beings are blessed with five senses for the detection of external stimuli;

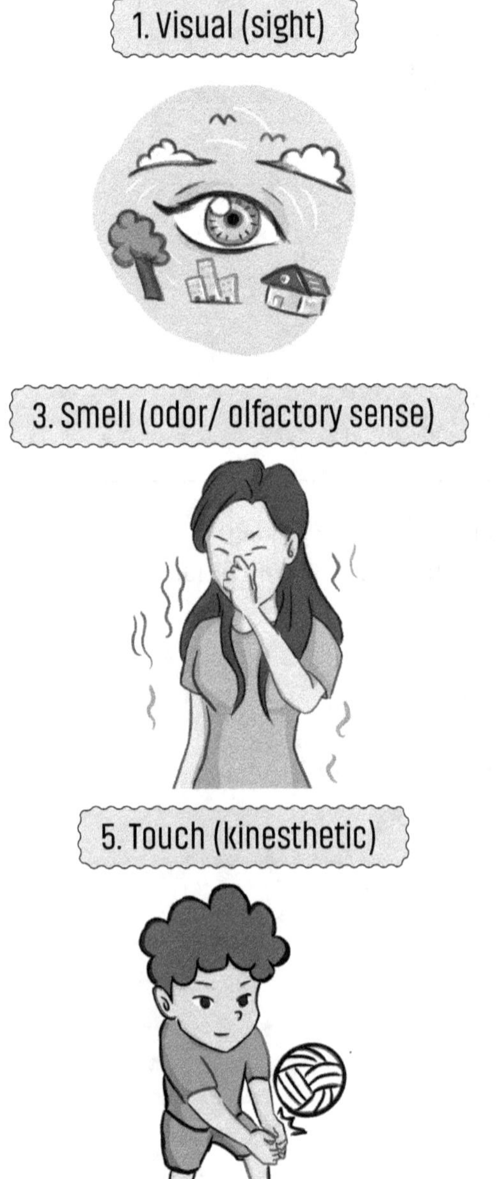

Examples of Stimuli:

Internal Stimuli (Coming from Inside)	External Stimuli (Coming from the environment)
Stream of thoughts	Light
Image/ daydream/ dream and flashback	Sound
Emotions (anger, sadness etc.)	Temperature
Any physiological experience (pounding heart, sweating etc.)	Taste
	Odor
	Seasonal/ climatic changes
	Any situation (school, examination hall, bus, public place, home etc.)

The mentioned stimuli can trigger human-beings and they can respond to them in a variety of ways. These ways could be silent or loud, expressive or inexpressive, ethical or unethical and rational or irrational. It solely depends on the ways by which an individual "thinks" and upon considering its thinking as an absolute reality how the individual reacts.

Activity Time (2.2)

How will you respond in the following situations?

Please fill out the following worksheet;

S. No.	Situations	Responses
1.	Your exams are approaching and you are not prepared.	
2.	Your teacher is scolding you in front of the whole class.	
3.	Somebody is bullying you.	
4.	A stranger is stalking you.	

S. No.	Situations	Responses
5.	You won a gold medal in a chess competition.	
6.	You had a nightmare.	
7.	There were heavy snowfalls and as a result you had a severe cold.	
8.	There was a severe thunderstorm.	
9.	You have to face your parents/ guardian after doing something unethical.	
10.	You get an "F" grade in your science exam.	

Now let's move to the last concept, which is the basic cognitive model.

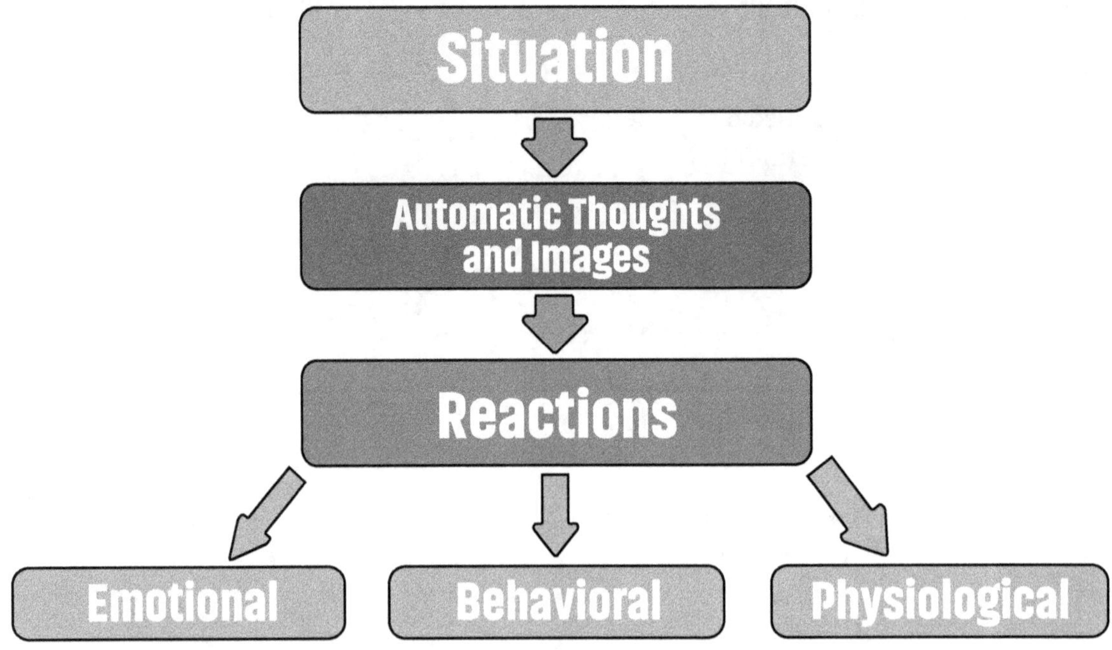

The basic cognitive model has six components;

1. Situation:

It could be any upcoming situation, any current situation, or any situation after the event/ incident where an individual is reflecting on what happened.

2. Automatic Thoughts and Images:

Thoughts and images that are beyond voluntary control pop up in the blink of an eye or like a flashlight are called automatic thoughts and images. Some people think in terms of thoughts, whereas others think through images. Thinking through images is conceptualized as thinking through mental pictures. Some people think through thoughts and images collectively.

3. Reactions:

Reactions are of three kinds; emotional, behavioral, and physiological, which are also known as bodily reactions. Some emotional reactions include sadness, depression, grief, anxiety, happiness, anger, joy, and nostalgia. Some behavioral reactions include blaming, criticizing, isolating from people, escaping from situations, crying, and shouting. Some physiological reactions include difficulty in breathing, difficulty in swallowing, butterflies in the stomach, palpitations, sweating, vertigo, tremors, and nervousness.

As per the basic cognitive model, the situation is not directly responsible for the reaction. It is automatic thoughts and images that are responsible for the reactions. We carry these thoughts and images everywhere with us, but unfortunately, we are not aware of them the same way we are aware of our reactions. This awareness is more dominant, it bypasses the awareness related to our automatic thoughts and images, and we draw the final conclusion by analyzing and blaming the situation only. In any situation, there is a need to hold ourselves and get the awareness of our automatic thoughts and images. We need to think and reflect on the messages we are continuously giving to ourselves. We need to identify our self-dialogue. Current psychologists call this 'internal dialogue.' The techniques to identify automatic thoughts and images will be discussed in chapter 4.

Solving Together

George, a fifth-grade student, says he is not interested in studying anything. He adds that he is not even interested in opening a book. He explains that by doing so, he experiences sadness and palpitations.

What kind of automatic thoughts/ images and reactions would there be in this scenario?

Automatic Thoughts/ Images	Reactions
George's automatic thoughts could be; • "I am unable to do so." • "I am incompetent." • "School is difficult." • "The teacher does not appreciate my efforts." • "The syllabus/ contents are difficult to understand." George's automatic images could be; • Seeing himself weak. • Seeing himself tiny and others big, as big as a dinosaur. • Seeing himself as a powerless student. • Seeing himself drowning in a river. • Seeing school as a haunted house.	George's psychological reaction is sadness. George's physiological reaction is palpitations.

Activity Time (2.3)

Now, how would you respond to the following situations?

What would your automatic thoughts/ images be?

What would be your emotional, physiological, and behavioral reactions?

Please fill out the following worksheet;

S. No.	Situations	Automatic Thoughts/ Images	Emotional Reactions	Physiological Reactions	Behavioral Reactions
1.	Your exams are approaching and you are not prepared.				
2.	Your teacher is scolding you in front of the whole class.				

S. No.	Situations	Automatic Thoughts/ Images	Emotional Reactions	Physiological Reactions	Behavioral Reactions
3.	Somebody is bullying you.				
4.	A stranger is stalking you.				
5.	You won a gold medal in a chess competition.				
6.	You had a nightmare.				
7.	There were heavy snowfalls, and as a result, you had a severe cold.				
8.	There was a severe thunderstorm.				
9.	You have to face your parents/ guardian after doing something unethical.				
10.	You get an "F" grade on your science exam.				

As per Cognitive Behavioral Therapy (CBT), humans are born with a blueprint that makes them think. Each one of us thinks as thinking helps to predict and understand the self, situations, others, and the world. You can observe other people who think differently and behave differently from you in the same situation. You may enjoy yourself by watching a particular movie, whereas someone around you may not like that movie, or maybe that person is not interested in movies at all. It completely depends on the way a person thinks, feels, and perceives. Similarly, some people seem logical to you, whereas others may seem illogical. This is how CBT conceptualizes the psychological functioning of humans. CBT conceptualizes, diagnoses, and manages psychological problems in a cognitive way. It believes that there is always a set of thinking patterns, psychologically termed as cognitive errors, which yields various kinds of psychological problems. This will be explained more in chapter 4. Since we all dwell in the past, worry about the future, deflect in the present, and are thinking organisms, it can be concluded that CBT is beneficial for all of us. It is a global demand as it focuses on thinking patterns, and it holds a premise that is; "The way we think is the way we feel, and the way we feel is the way we behave."

Activity Time (2.4)

Name any three people who think differently from you.	Name any three people who think similarly to you.
1.	1.
2.	2.
3.	3.

Please fill out the following worksheet;

	What thinking patterns makes them different from you?
People who think differently from you.	A.
	B.
	C.
	What thinking patterns makes them similar to you?
People who think similarly to you	A.
	B.
	C.

CHAPTER 3: Me with A Battery

Let's start the chapter with the following questions;

- Have you ever seen a battery?
- Do you know how a battery works?
- Do you know how a battery drains?
- Are you aware of a battery inside you?
- Do you know how your internal battery works?
- Is the internal battery chargeable and/ or rechargeable?
- Can you explain to someone how your internal battery is drained?

You really need to understand these "battery" related concepts so that you may get the most out of Cognitive Behavioral Therapy (CBT) in your daily life.

A lot of events and activities are going on in your daily life. You wake up early in the morning, get fresh, have cereals for breakfast, go to school and carry out a number of academic and sports activities at school. You come back home and do a lot of things. Some of you read and write, while others watch TV. Similarly, some go for music and dancing classes, while others go for sports classes. Each one of you has hobbies and interests to share that keep you busy and stop you from mischief.

Activity Time (3.1)

Share your hobbies and interests that keep you busy.

Please fill out the following worksheet;

(You may take help from the list of hobbies and interests given next to this worksheet).

S. No.	Hobbies and interests
1.	
2.	
3.	

S. No.	Hobbies and interests
4.	
5.	
6.	
7.	
8.	
9.	
10.	

S. No.	Hobbies	Activities
1.	Creative hobbies	Watercolors and crafting like drawing, card making, and painting.
2.	Physical hobbies	All kinds of sports activities like yoga, tai chi, running, darts, soccer, basketball, badminton, and all such games.
3.	Mental hobbies	Reading, writing, Sudoku, crossword puzzles, jigsaw puzzles, and learning a new language.
4.	Musical hobbies	Singing, dancing, joining a choir, learning to play a musical instrument, learning about different musicians and music genres, learning to write lyrics, and listening to music.
5.	Collecting hobbies	Collecting books, clothes, toys, candles, autographed pictures or other items, sports equipment, and event tickets.
6.	Food/ Drink hobbies	Cooking, baking, and grilling.
7.	Games/ puzzles hobbies	Online and video games.

S. No.	Questions	Status
		YES NO
1.	Have you ever noticed your feelings and mental state while carrying out your hobbies?	☑ ☒

If yes, explain your feelings and mental state. How did your hobbies affect your mood, energy levels, sleep, appetite, and overall well-being?

S. No.	Questions	Status
2.	Do you think that your hobbies serve to be a healthy distractor for you?	YES ☐ NO ☐

If yes, highlight the events/ situations that you think are managed by your hobbies.

S. No.	Questions	Status
3.	Have you ever noticed that your hobbies bring any kind of social change?	YES ☐ NO ☐

If yes, highlight the social change. How have others benefited from your hobbies?

or

What kind of healthy social relationships have you formed (or strengthened) through your hobbies?

S. No.	Questions	Status
4.	Do you think you can maintain your health and fitness through your hobbies?	YES ☐ NO ☐

If yes, explain how this can be achieved.

S. No.	Questions	Status
5.	Do you believe that your hobbies will affect or bring a change in your personality?	YES ☐ NO ☐

If yes, explain how your hobbies could potentially change your personality.

Readers who marked "yes" and explained most of the questions accordingly are more likely to grasp the "battery" concept. Those readers who marked "no" to most of the questions have to revise and practice the basic cognitive model explained in chapter #2 of this book.

Have you ever seen the following?

This is a device which is known as a battery. It is used to store energy for later use. It has two terminals/ sides; one is positive, while the other is negative. A battery stores chemical energy and converts it into electrical energy. The life of a battery depends on its use - how often it is used, how frequently it is charged, which is the number of times a battery is charged in a day, week, month, or year and the degree of electric current used to charge a battery. Electric current should match the capacity of a battery. An electric current that is too low or too high would negatively affect the functioning of a battery.

There are different kinds of batteries, with different storage capacities, manufactured for different purposes. A battery would remain functional (healthy) for a number of years if its use and charging ratio are equal, it is not overcharged, and only the required degree of electric current is passed that is in the best match with its capacity.

Without a doubt, you cannot imagine a world without a battery. Think about the following gadgets without a battery, realistically speaking, without energy;

Laptop

Tablet

Mobile phone

Digital cameras

Handheld video game consoles

Artificial limbs and hearing aids

Automobiles and industrial trucks like forklifts

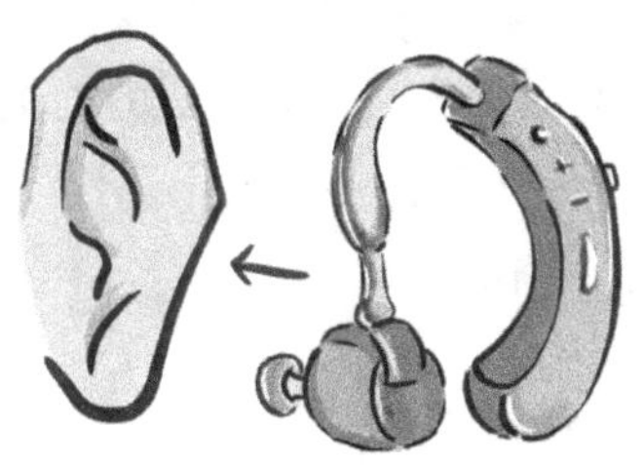

- What would happen to all the downloaded apps and games if your devices were out of battery?

- How would digital cameras work without a battery?

- How would people with artificial limbs or hearing aids function if their gadgets were without batteries?

- How would you set off on a long journey if your automobile is without a battery?

- How would people build beautiful towns and buildings if tractors, graders, bulldozers, and excavators are without batteries?

Conclusion

Of course, in the current era, we cannot live without batteries. They are used everywhere, in each part of the globe. A world without batteries would be like the dark ages, where we would all be very limited in terms of knowledge, mobility, economic growth and progress, relationships, and lifestyle.

 How does a battery drain?

Let's take the example of a smartphone battery. A smartphone battery drains due to the following reasons;

- The screen is used at a bright level for a continuous period of time.
- Numerous apps are running in the background, which is of no use.
- The Smartphone is used for long hours for calls, browsing the internet, or playing games.
- The charger is not giving the required amount of electric current to the battery.
- Extreme temperature variations can affect the battery.

It is worth highlighting that a smartphone battery drains fast if the aforementioned reasons are prolonged, for example;

- The screen is used at a bright level for a continuous period of time.
- Numerous apps are running in the background, which is of no use.
- The battery is exposed to direct sunlight.

Let's play some true and false.

Mark a tick ✓ if you feel the statement fits with you, and mark a cross ✗ if you feel the statement is not related to you;

Please fill out the following worksheet;

S. No.	Statements	My Responses	
1.	You have some energy storage inside you, like a battery.	☐	☒
2.	Your energy storage drains due to some events and situations.	☐	☒
3.	Your energy storage drains due to your thinking patterns.	☐	☒

S. No.	Statements	My Responses
4.	Your energy storage can be charged/ recharged.	☐ ☐
5.	You don't know how to charge/ re-charge your internal energy storage.	☐ ☐
6.	There are some activities that can charge your internal battery.	☐ ☐
7.	When your battery drains, you experience unpleasant/ unwanted emotions like sadness, boredom, anger and disgust.	☐ ☐
8.	A lot of things are going on at the back of your mind (like multiple background apps of a smartphone), which is indirectly affecting your emotions and mood.	☐ ☐
9.	You can function without energy or internal energy storage.	☐ ☐
10.	If the internal battery is charged, it can positively impact your sleep, mood, and overall well-being.	☐ ☐

Please fill out the following;

1. You get a chocolate.

What facial expression would suit this situation?

2. You stood first in the class.

What facial expression would suit this situation?

3. You are scolded by your teacher.

What facial expression would suit this situation?

4. You had a nightmare.

What facial expression would suit this situation?

5. You visit a park of your choice.

What facial expression would suit this situation?

6. You are allowed to keep any pet of your choice.

What facial expression would suit this situation?

7. Somebody is calling you bad names.

What facial expression would suit this situation?

8. You think you will not get good grades in your exams.

What facial expression would suit this situation?

9. You think and plan to celebrate your birthday in the best café in town.

What facial expression would suit this situation?

10. You dream that you are at your favorite theme park.

What facial expression would suit this situation?

By solving the worksheets of this chapter, you identified and explained the impact of hobbies in your daily life. You understood the working of a battery, and I expect you developed an idea that you, too, carry a battery. This battery is internal, chargeable, and rechargeable. Like that of a smartphone, or other batteries, this battery also drains. It drains when it is used. It drains fast when it is used excessively and purposelessly and is not charged well, and is not recharged when required.

I would like to give you a piece of advice. You need to be careful about the signs of your "battery drain." Signs of battery drain are as follows;

- ☛ Feeling irritable without any logical reason.
- ☛ Experiencing an unceasing episode of anger in a minor situation.
- ☛ Having sleep difficulties without any medical cause.
- ☛ Eating too much or too little.
- ☛ Indigestion or an upset stomach.
- ☛ Nausea.
- ☛ Sadness and hopelessness without any factual reason.
- ☛ Feeling sleepy or fatigued and sluggish without doing much work.
- ☛ The anxiousness is really hard to control.
- ☛ Having a strong feeling that others are untrustworthy.
- ☛ Having a lack of trust in social relationships.
- ☛ You do not want to go to school.
- ☛ Your body aches without any marked stressor or injury.
- ☛ You have butterflies in your stomach.
- ☛ You have a strong feeling that life is full of boredom and unpleasantness.

When you experience the above-mentioned sign(s), first think about the following figure;

Secondly, hold on to yourself and ask yourself the following questions;

- What kind of situations/ events have I frequently faced in the last seven days/ fourteen days/ a month or six months?
- What do I think in those situations?
- What do I conclude from those situations?
- How do I cope with the situations I am frequently facing?
- Can I reduce the frequency of situations I have faced in the last seven days/ fourteen days/ a month, or six months?
- Can I change my thinking patterns and conclusions that I have drawn through those situations?
- Shall I identify and carry out my hobbies and interests to charge/ recharge my internal battery?
- Can I share my thoughts and feelings with any trustworthy person in my immediate surroundings?

These questions will help you to identify the areas/ situations which are draining your internal battery, and you will be able to find ways to stop this "battery drain" or the "fast drain." Moreover, you will be able to develop and carry out certain things where you will be charging and recharging your battery just at the right time.

Thirdly, remember that your internal storage is completely under your control. You can either maintain it or break it. You must take full responsibility for it. For reference, see the responses you marked under activity 3.4. It can be concluded that exposure to some situations, pleasurable/ rewarding activities, and certain thinking patterns can positively impact your feelings and overall well-being.

Repeated exposure to rewarding and pleasing situations will keep you charged, positive and productive as compared to the opposite. Of course, you will not feel happy and positive when you have to repeatedly go through situations in which you are criticized, scolded, and punished.

In your daily life, you can do a lot of things to keep your battery charged. For better clarification kindly go through the following;

1.	Always eat healthily. You should follow Horrid Henry – Healthy Eating Episode for details.
2.	Make sure you take adequate sleep.
3.	Develop healthy social relationships – relationships that make you feel good about yourself.
4.	Make a healthy routine – a routine where you divide your time between different activities.
5.	Develop hobbies and interests. Make sure you carry them out every day to some extent.

6.	Spend time with your family/ caretakers.
7.	Go on a holiday/ vacation.
8.	Give your best at school, home, and everywhere else.
9.	Never blame, criticize or punish yourself.
10.	Practice a healthy self-dialogue – a dialogue where you appreciate yourself even for a minor effort you put into a task/ activity. In the case where you make mistakes, say to yourself something like, "It's just a mistake. I did my best, and in the future, I will try not to repeat my mistakes."
11.	Incorporate the feedback given by your parents, teachers, and other significant relationships so that you may grow your personality.
12.	Spare some time where you help others. It could be any individual or a group like special children and/ or a marginalized community.
13.	Learn to forgive others for their mistakes.
14.	Understand diversity. It is the understanding of the fact that people come from different cultural backgrounds, so they have different attitudes and behaviors. Their norm could be abnormal for you and vice versa.
15.	Practice religiosity/ spirituality as per your religious values.

Human beings are the only creatures who are blessed with mental functions like thinking, reasoning, perceiving, foreseeing, and planning. They have developed a certain way of thinking and believing on the basis of some experiences. Some patterns of thinking may become "unrealistic," but the individual can consider it as an "absolute reality." So, human beings are affected by situations as it shapes and/ or cultivate different themes of thinking patterns in them. So, it is healthy to keep a record of the situations they are facing and the styles of thinking they are continuously developing out of it. These thinking patterns can be strengthened and can become very concrete through repeated experiences and without managing it in time. All this is discussed in chapter # 4 of this book.

You can change the impact of a situation(s) by changing your state in the situation or the situation itself. Some examples are as follows;

➥ You can relieve your boredom by reading a book or going out to play.

➥ You can control your anger by leaving the situation or by distracting yourself through imagery, deep breathing, or simply shifting your thinking to something else.

➥ In the case of self-blaming and self-critical inner dialogue, you may shift to an alternate and/ or self-appreciating dialogue by counting your minor to major achievements of the day. Also, you can engage yourself in an activity in a different situation.

Believe in the fact, there is a battery inside of you that is completely under your control. You can use it, enhance it, charge/ recharge it, and prevent it from a useless drain, fast drain, and permanent damage through your decisions, opinions, and daily life choices that you make in different situations.

Your Fault, My Fault

Are you familiar with the "crowning achievement of evolution?" Mental health professionals of the current era name this "cortical evolution." This concept states that the human brain is very special. Now two questions arise, "What makes the human brain special?" and "How is the human brain special?" You must carefully go through this chapter in order to get the answer.

Activity Time (4.1)

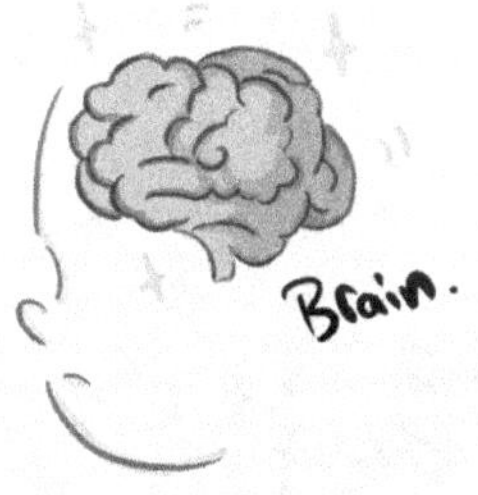

? Have you ever seen a human brain?

Please share your understanding below;

Activity Time (4.2)

? Have you ever seen a book?

What does a book look like in terms of color, shape, size, and volume?

Please share your understanding below;

"Don't judge a book by its cover" – A famous metaphorical phrase that is often used to explain that one should not judge or conclude the worth of anything by its external structure and/ or appearance.

S. No.	Questions	Your Answers
1.	How does he/she communicate with you and others?	
2.	How does he/she plan his/her daily life activities?	
3.	What is his/her favorite subject?	
4.	What are his/ her hobbies?	

S. No.	Questions	Your Answers
5.	How does he/she prepare for school exams?	
6.	Who is brave among you and what makes you or your friend brave?	
7.	How does your friend make decisions? Do they make them alone or by involving others?	
8.	Who can better memorize any new piece of information among you?	
9.	Who learned or who can better learn any new skill (like cycling) among you?	
10.	Who is more outward and social among you and why is that so?	

The above questions cover several higher mental functions like language, thinking, planning, deciding, emotions, learning, memory, and socialization that are controlled by the brain. Each mental function is carried out by a specific region in the brain. A human brain is not a muscle or an elastic band; it is an organ that contains nerves and blood vessels. A human brain is made up of water and salts, which make it a jelly-like organ with multiple bumps and grooves enclosed in the skull. A human brain is judged by these bumps and grooves (details are further mentioned in this chapter).

Activity Time (4.4)

Recall yourself during infancy (0-1 years).

Please fill out the worksheet;

S. No.	Questions	Your Answers
1.	What was the size of your body when you were born?	
2.	Were you able to execute functions like talking, reading, and writing during infancy? If not, what kind of functions/ activities were you able to perform during infancy?	
3.	What was the first word you uttered properly?	

S. No.	Questions	Your Answers
4.	In which month did you start to crawl?	
5.	In which month did you stand without aid?	
6.	Were you able to dress and undress without aid during infancy? If not, explain the reason behind this.	
7.	How did you explain needs like hunger, thirst, and sleep to others during infancy?	
8.	At what age did you solve a simple mathematical operation like 2+2 or 10-4?	
9.	At what age did you start to eat and drink independently (without any aid)?	
10.	At what age did you start to bathe individually (without any aid)?	

A brain of an infant weighs 400 grams which are equal to a small loaf of bread or a soft drink in a can. It gains weight with the passage of time as infants continuously attempt to learn multiple functions, for example, focusing on vision and exploring the surroundings. This brain development is continuous as the infant is continuously under multiple learning processes like language, memory, thinking, and reasoning. The time period during which language develops is very sensitive as it involves listening, understanding, and identifying people in their surroundings by their names and unique identities. At this stage, an infant undergoes emotional development, too, as he/she develops certain attachment patterns and bonds of love and trust with his/her caregivers. The way the caregivers hold, smile, cuddle and play with an infant lays the foundation of certain ways of thinking patterns, decisions, and the ways by which an infant will interact with others later in life.

Mental health professionals, along with the aforementioned factors, highlight the role of nutrition, exposure to toxins and microorganisms (infections and diseases) in the environment, and experiences gained through social relationships in the development of the brain. All these factors affect the shape and design of the appearance of the brain. All these lay the foundation, a blueprint or navigation of certain thinking styles, decision-making styles, attachment patterns, and dealing with social relationships in later life. All this is elusive in nature, which means that infinite variables/ factors continuously impact our brain development which is broadly classified as what we discussed in chapter two of this book, bio-psychosocial variables. Some of the variables have been discovered, while others are still hidden from scientists and researchers worldwide, for example, numerous variants of bacteria, viruses, and fungi are still unknown to mankind, and the degree of impact they can bring on mankind's brain development and overall well-being is still covert. Similarly, the impact of numerous psychosocial variables too is covert, like, how the use of technology is changing the bumps and grooves of our brain, how the globalized world and culture are affecting our brain and mind (mental functions), ideas, thoughts, social relationships and, above of all, our reasoning and decision-making. Mental health professionals of the current era conclude it as;

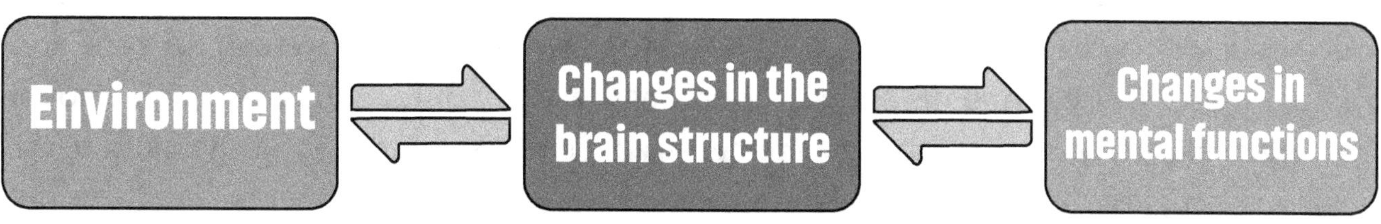

This conclusion is a "two-way street." The environment affects our brain covering, the brain structure, which further affects/ impacts our mental functions and altogether, through these mental functions, we create an impact in the environment, i.e., how we understand a social construct and act accordingly, for example, "boys are brave and extroverted" so a boy will be more social, outgoing and he will be participating in outdoor activities. On the contrary, "girls are sensitive and introverted" so a girl will have a few social relationships and she will participate more in closed-door games, unlike a boy. This is how the world continuously influences, shapes, and designs our brain regions in which mental operations reside, and they collectively influence and affect the environment in several ways. For example, in one situation, we are annoyed and relaxed in the other one.

Similarly, chatting with some people yields positivity and happiness, whereas other people make us frustrated and angry. These emotions and behaviors are not something that mankind is born with. Of course, brain structures are there, but they are "blank" – nothing is pre-stored. Functions/ skills like "what to do" and "how to do" in any situation come from the environment, which is known as "nurturing." Nurturing is a continuous and lifelong process as it emerges from the immediate (primary) environment where you were born, from this environment it moves to your maternal and paternal relatives, especially the elders of the family, school teachers, friends, acquaintances, role models, and the mass media. You learn from all these sources; your brain structures are changed, and you act accordingly.

Human beings keep on learning new things, and brain structures are constantly changing. The bumps and grooves change. Either they will increase in number, or the existing ones will become dense and deep. In some cases, some bumps and grooves and certain brain regions degenerate as a result of trauma that can be due to bullying and harassment, domestic violence, physical and/ or sexual abuse, exposure to toxic environments, and much more. This continuous and never-ending elasticity of the human brain is known as brain plasticity or what current mental health professionals around the globe refer to as 'neuroplasticity.' In a nutshell, brain structures (or brain regions) change with the passage of time because of diverse environmental influences and/ or exposures. This is brain plasticity. When you learn something new and keep on rehearsing and repeating it at different times, the bumps and grooves will become dense and deep, which further will enhance your brain regions. On the contrary, if you learn something new but do not rehearse or revise it, then it will be more likely that you will forget it. Why is that so? Because you did not allow your brain to change its structure, you did not allow it to stretch, change and design its structure and you did not allow enhancement of the brain regions.

The entire mankind has a brain that apparently looks similar, but, logically speaking, the number of bumps and grooves are entirely different due to different environmental exposures. Modern-day scientists and researchers also highlight the role of personal choices and decisions that significantly influence your brain. Let's discuss a few examples;

➡ You decided to go to bed early so that you may get up early.

➡ You decided to study for an exam instead of going out to a birthday party.

➡ You made a decision to exercise daily and people around you are not in favor of it.

➡ Arthur prefers a balanced diet whereas his sister prefers chocolates over everything.

➡ Amelia decides to read a novel to manage her stress, whereas her sister Mia prefers to listen to music.

This is "the crowning achievement of evolution" alias "cortical evolution." You are blessed with a brain that is flexible, elastic, and unstoppable, which means that you can acquire/ learn billions of new pieces of information and skills ranging from self-care to carrying out complex.

Functions like safely landing a plane. In addition, cognitive functions that include; thinking (and higher-order thinking), reasoning, and deciding also come under "the crowning achievement of evolution." These functions make each of us "human" and superior to all other species on earth. The way we learn, plan, think, decide, feel and express our emotions is entirely different from other mammals and species. These unique capabilities make humans an "ever-green" creature and carry invincible reign over all creatures of the planet. Numerous animals like dinosaurs, dodos, Tasmanian tigers, and woolly mammoths are extinct now due to the lack of a brain like humans and the absence of unique cognitive functions. The brain and the cognitive functions that we are blessed with help us to decide, adapt and survive. That is why the human brain is special, and the factors that are explained above make it special.

Now we need to investigate another matter, where do things go wrong? Who is responsible for our unpleasant and unwanted emotions and feelings like sadness, depression, anxiety, frustration, irritability, and anger? On the contrary, what makes us experience joy, serenity, hope, amusement, and awe? Yes, it is the brain and cognitive functions. If you really want to identify the culprit, a responsible figure that is creating problems for you in your daily life or makes you feel aversive about yourself, others, the world, and the future - are the microorganisms in your thinking and perception or what is also known as the "dirty tricks" that your cognitive functions (mind) are playing with you. There are at least twelve kinds of "dirty tricks" that your mind can play with you. It can convince you of those facts and perceptions which actually don't exist, but your mind just convinces you of them as you take them as an "absolute truth." So, beware of the following "dirty tricks";

S. No.	Dirty Tricks	Definitions
1.	One-Eyed Ogre	Seeing things from only one perspective and ignoring all other perspectives and alternatives.
2.	Prisoner of Feeling	Using your feelings as the main guide for your actions and thoughts. You say, "You are right because you feel you are right."
3.	Disaster Forecaster	Falsely believing something awful will happen, but you have no realistic (empirical) evidence to back up your ideas and conclusions.
4.	Maxi-Me Thinking	Falsely believing that it is only you who is responsible for all bad things and misfortunes that happen to you or other people.
5.	Lame Blaming	You use the labels for yourself ("I'm bad") and/or others ("She's a witch, and it is all her fault.").
6.	Mules Rules	Stubbornly insisting, without any logic and rationality, that your thoughts and ideas about how you, other people, and the world are true and accurate. Everybody should behave according to your rules.
7.	Countless Thinking	Continuously and incorrectly convincing yourself that strengths, successes, and good experiences do not count. Only "failures" count in life.

S. No.	Dirty Tricks	Definitions
8.	Tragic Magic Thinking	Incorrectly believing that you know exactly what is going through someone else's mind. You take it as an "absolute" conclusion, and you don't check out or ask the person for confirmation and/ or clarification.
9.	Tall-Tale Thinking	You just believe in something despite there being little to back up the idea and the entire belief system.
10.	No Middle Riddle	Seeing and concluding things in a too broad and rigid way, like 'you are perfect' or 'you are a total loser.'
11.	Circus Mirror Thinking	When you look at yourself, other people, or what happens to you, you shrink (minimize) the positive (+) and/ or supersize (maximize) the negative (−).
12.	Too Fast Forward	You jump to big conclusions and decisions by using small and incomplete bits of information. You don't wait to get all the results, information, and a clear picture that you need before coming to a conclusion.

Maintain a diary to identify the dirty tricks discussed above

Please fill out the following worksheet;

Date	Situation	Emotion (Feeling)	Thought	Dirty Trick

By now, you must be aware of the concepts related to situations, thoughts, feelings, and dirty tricks, so you should be easily able to fill out the worksheet. Through this worksheet, you will be able to identify the real evil-doer who creates problems for you in your daily life, and thus a firm conclusion will be reached whether it is your fault or other people's fault for your problems, mishaps, and misfortunes.

I Need You at Home

Home is the house or flat that you live in, especially with your family.

"A family is a socially recognised group that forms an emotional bond among its members and functions as an economic unit of society. Typically, families are linked by blood, marriage, cohabitation, or adoption."

 Are you living with your family?

In the case of "NO," elaborate on why you are not living with your family.

Please use the following to share your answer;

In the case of "YES," explain the best part about living with your family.

Please use the following to share your answer;

? Do you think there are some emotional and behavioral problems in your family?

In the case of "YES," elaborate on the kind of emotional and behavioral problems prevalent in your family dynamic.

Please use the following to share your answer;

In the case of "NO," elaborate on the kind of thinking and communication patterns, attitudes, and behaviors that are making your family a "problem-free" or an "ideal" family.

Please use the following to share your answer;

Think about yourself – "Your Real Self" and answer the following worksheet.

Please fill out the worksheet;

S. No.	Questions	Your Answers
1.	To what extent do you feel satisfied and happy or dissatisfied and sad with your family? Also, explain the factors that make you feel that way.	
2.	What makes your family a source of comfort or discomfort for you?	
3.	How does your family provide you with a secure or insecure base where you can share or cannot share your daily life stressors and problems?	
4.	Explain why (or why not) you are attached to your family.	

S. No.	Questions	Your Answers
5.	In what ways are you grateful or ungrateful that you are blessed with a family?	
6.	What do you think about those people who don't have a family?	
7.	With whom do you think you are attached the most in the family and why? If it is nobody then explain why you are not attached to anybody in the family.	
8.	What would your life be like without a family?	
9.	What are some of your strengths you think are due to your family?	
10.	What are some of the factors that connect you to your parents and siblings, or what disconnects you from them?	

S. No.	Questions	Your Answers
11.	How does your family protect (or not protect) you from the stressors, problems, and challenges of daily life?	
12.	What does your family teach you about norms – the sense of right and wrong?	
13.	What makes you think that your parents are available or unavailable for you?	
14.	How do you express your emotional distress, pain, and suffering? Do you express it among your family? Explain your "YES" or "NO" answer.	
15.	Explain your attachment style with your family. Is it a secure, insecure, or ambivalent attachment style?	

A family serves the following functions;

Socializing children

A family is a major unit that is responsible to fulfill children's social needs like that of hunger, thirst, and shelter. A child will not be able to communicate and express themself if his/her social needs are not met. Parents, grandparents, siblings, and other significant relatives socialize with children to enhance their brain development and foster their relationships. This process begins at the time a child is born.

Provides practical and social support

Food, clothes, shelter, and a basic sense of warmth and security come from a family. A child develops closeness, secure attachment, and a sense of connectedness if he/she gets comfort, love, support, and practical solutions at times of emotional distress and problems.

Social identity

Religion, race, ethnicity, and the social class of a child are determined by a family as he/she acquires it through parents. Today you are able to tell your race, religion, and social class because you know about it through your parents and family. Think of those people who don't have a family. Can they talk about their race and ethnicity?

Teaching norms

In terms of communication, you know what to say, when to speak, where to speak, and in which kind of situations silence is required. Interrupting people, especially elders, while they are talking is considered bad. Following rules and regulations, like taking permission before entering a room and greetings, are considered good. This sense of right and wrong or do's and dont's come from the family as family is the first and the basic institution where a child learns norms and later executes them in different situations.

Do you think all families carry out the above-mentioned functions discussed?

In the case of "YES", explain your answer through an example of yourself, your friend, or any acquaintance.

Please use the following to share your answer;

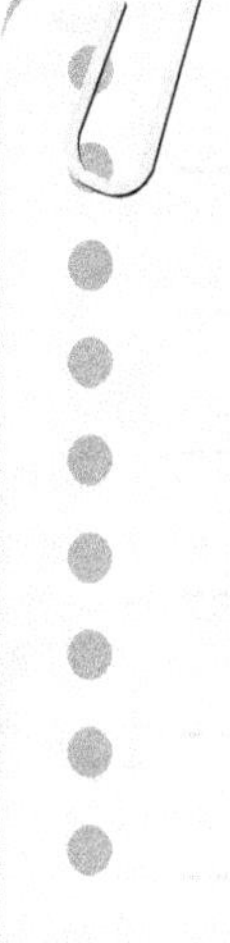

Where do things go wrong?

Things for a child and the family as a whole can be miserable due to the following reasons;

1.	Parents (or caregivers) are continuously struggling to meet the basic biological needs of the family to such a degree that children's psychological and social needs are compromised.
2.	Stress in the family due to financial issues, unemployment, and housing problems.
3.	Caregivers (or parents) are too busy in their lives, and they don't have time for their children, especially for their emotional needs.
4.	Parents, both, or any one of them is suffering from emotional-behavioral problems, a disability, or a medical ailment.

5.	When children repeatedly witness harsh arguments, sarcasm, and/ or violence among parents and significant elders.
6.	Separation and/ or divorce are witnessed by the children.
7.	Authoritarian parents/ caregivers who expect a lot from their children with little responsiveness and very little to no support and warmth.
8.	Enmeshed relationships and/ or disengaged relationships are there among other family members.
9.	Children not accepting step-parents and/ or step-siblings.
10.	Gender inequality.
11.	Lack of a support system.
12.	Child abuse, neglect, and abandonment.
13.	Lack of proper communication between the parents and children, siblings, and other relatives.
14.	There is a family atmosphere consisting of arguments and justifications all the time.
15.	Foster care.

As per United Nations (2022), the global human population is 8.0 billion. Without a doubt, we can conclude that 8.0 billion people are diverse as they belong to different families and hold diverse cultural backgrounds, races, and ethnicities. Likewise, entire mankind would carry different views of life due to different ways of thinking, reasoning, and perceiving events and situations in life. The same diversity could be witnessed in the context of a family;

- Some people would consider family as a socially recognized group and on the contrary, some would consider it a threat to their self and unique identity.

- Some individuals can feel a strong emotional connection to their family members, while others may experience pain and disappointment.

- Few people can proudly claim, "I am nothing without my family." On the other hand, a group of people can say, "I am unique and versatile without my family."

- You can discover many people belonging to different age groups who feel secure with their families. For them, their families are like a harbor where they can anchor safely. Conversely, you could discover a lot of people on this planet who could be going through intense hopelessness, agony, and misery only because of their families.

Activity Time (5.5)

Compare and contrast.

S. No.	What can I achieve in the future because of the support of my family?	What is holding me back from achieving in the future because of my family?

Due to any reason, if a family fails to serve its functions or a child is not able to establish and maintain a bond of love, warmth, secure attachment, and a sense of belongingness with its family members, then a child can develop a host of emotional-behavioral problems that are stated as follows;

- Lying
- Defiance
- Excessive screen time
- Eating problems/ disorders
- Impulsive, aggressive behaviors and addictive disorders
- Bedtime behavior problems like bedtime resistance
- Temper Tantrums
- School refusal
- Truancy
- Bullying
- Chronic sadness and hopelessness
- Generalized fear, anxiety, or depression
- Excessively living in isolation
- Distrust in family and social relationships
- Personality problems

If you perceive that your family is a source of comfort and overall well-being, then you are one of the luckiest and most blessed among earth's 8.0 billion population. But what about the rest? Can you recall what was discussed in the previous chapters? We discussed that we, as humans, are not alike. We are diverse and distinct from one another. Yes, we may look alike, but from the inside, it is like we are carrying an independent universe that is full of diverse experiences, thinking styles, beliefs, pain, and emotional wounds.

Getting hurt by your own family or any significant family member is devastating. It brings a lot of emotional distress, self-critical (self-destructive) thoughts, and/ or destructive thoughts about others. These wounds are emotional that can deeply affect your perception of yourself, others, and the entire world. The scars of these wounds may persist forever if they are not timely identified and managed. This mechanism of pain and suffering is entirely different from that of physical injuries, which could be detected through laboratory and radiology tests and, therefore, can be treated through medication and/ or physiotherapy. The emotional distress that stems from family problems is not that easy to identify and manage, both for the sufferer and the psychotherapist. Specifically talking about the sufferer, identifying and healing emotional-behavioral problems that have roots in family turmoil requires a lot of time, courage, stamina, and a daily life commitment as the damage is deep in the psyche of the sufferer. If you think and feel in a way that you were victimized by your family or any of the family members, then, along with the techniques explained in chapter # 3 of this book, you need to go through the following activities.

Identify your self-dialogue/ internal dialogue related to the family. Try your best to change that thought or make it less intense.

Please fill out the following worksheet;

S. No.	Statements I Say to Myself • What do I say to myself due to a bad experience with my family?	My Talk Back • What should be my actual response to the thoughts? • Is the existing thought healthy? • Shall I change the existing thought as it brings negative reactions?

Identify your aggressive (hot) thoughts related to the family and/or your sufferings.

Try your best to generate cool and relaxing thoughts that will help you to overcome your hot thoughts.

For example, Saoirse thinks that her family is authoritative, as nobody allows her to do anything she likes. She has to submit her wills and desires over that of her family's commands. All this makes her angry. These streams of thoughts are "hot" thoughts. Alternatively, she can think that she can do the stuff of her choice when she is at school or at a friend's house. These thoughts can make her calm. Thus they are "cool" thoughts.

Try for yourself now. Identify your hot thoughts and write them in the left column. Identify your cool thoughts and write them in the right column.

Please fill out the following worksheet;

S. No.	Hot Thoughts	Cool Thoughts

Manufacture emotional balms by asking certain questions to yourself, such as the following;

- What responsibility can I take to gain control over myself or to get out of this situation?

- Shall I learn to gain control over myself or to gain control over others? How shall I do it?

- Shall I learn to get rid of these unwanted and unpleasant emotions and feelings, or keep on showing aggression and cursing others? What strategy can I develop in either way?

- What am I really doing? Am I expecting others to come and heal me, or am I healing myself?

- Do I have a healthy thinking pattern and lifestyle to really come out of my adversities and situations?

These are some of the sample questions that you can ask yourself to identify your thinking patterns and check where you are currently standing in your life. Of course, you can develop a list of such questions (go through chapter no. 3). Depending on your findings. You can come up with strategies and ways through which you can overcome the troubles caused by your family.

Due to all of this, we need Cognitive Behavioral Therapy (CBT) at home. Please carefully go through the previous chapters to correctly apply CBT at home.

Chapter 6

I Need You For School

Do you know what school is?

A school is an institution for educating children.

Do you know how education is defined?

Education is the process of teaching, training, and learning that takes place in schools, colleges, or universities to improve knowledge and skills..

Activity Time (6.1)

Why do you go to school?

Please use the following to share your answer;

What do you like best about your school?

Please use the following to share your answer;

What do you hate the most about your school?

Please use the following to share your answer;

 Do you think it is important to go to school?

In the case of yes, elaborate on why school is important in an individual's life.

Please use the following to share your answer;

In the case of no, explain how the life of a person would be without school.

Please use the following to share your answer;

Activity Time (6.4)

Why would your friends go to school?

Please use the following to share your answer;

Why would your friends not go to school?

Please use the following to share your answer;

Activity Time (6.5)

Share your understanding of literacy and education. How are they similar, or how are they different?

Please use the following to share your answer;

I want you to think critically about the following;

- What is the purpose of education?

- Are schools really educating children?

- Why do a lot of schoolchildren suffer from psychological and behavioral problems?

- Why are some children anxious about going to school?

- In some children, there is a "battle of wills." They are unable to go to bed on time, and therefore they face a lot of trouble waking up early the next morning. Why is this?

Countries like Norway, Chile, Israel, and New Zealand spend billions of dollars on education, especially on school education. Why? Because they believe that education is key to development.

Do you believe that education is key to development?

YES   NO

Explain what made you mark "yes" or what made you mark "no".

Please use the following to share your answer;

Similarly, countries like Australia, the United States, and the United Kingdom spend a lot of money to give financial relief to students so that they may pursue education, at least basic education – primary education. Again, why are these countries doing this? You can observe numerous people around you who are enthusiastic about going to school. They want to pursue education because they think that through school, they will be able to learn a set of skills, build their character by sowing a set of values inside them, create a bright future for themselves and their loved ones and so they can be a pride for their country. We critically need to think to what extent this thinking pattern is true and what exactly validates this set of thoughts. But first, we need to see the following "ideal" purposes of education;

What did you conclude so far? Does the education system, particularly school education, serve the mentioned purposes? Why or why not? What about the fact that school children around the globe face a lot of learning, emotional, behavioral, and psychological disorders like that of teens and adults? The list of psychological issues that a lot of children, within the context of school, across the world go through are as follows;

➡ School refusal, truancy, and dropout.

➡ Eating problems/disorders.

➡ Anger and impulse-control problems.

➡ Poor relationships with teachers and other students.

➡ Deep mistrust of everybody in school.

➡ Anxiety disorders including generalized anxiety disorder, panic disorder, fear of evaluation, phobias, and performance anxiety.

- ➡ Learning disorders like dyslexia, dysgraphia, language processing disorder, and nonverbal learning disabilities.

- ➡ Conduct disorder.

- ➡ Autism.

- ➡ Attention-Deficit Hyperactivity Disorder (ADHD).

- ➡ Chemical addiction.

- ➡ Stress and anxiety related to exams.

- ➡ Self-confidence and self-esteem issues.

- ➡ Bullying or getting victimized by bullying and harassment.

- ➡ Poor self-concept and/ or identity crisis.

- ➡ Disruptive mood dysregulation disorder.

- ➡ Temper tantrums.

- ➡ Hostility, sadness, and depressive disorders.

- ➡ A strong unpleasant state as a consequence of biased, prejudiced, and discriminatory attitudes by teachers and/or students.

Activity Time (6.7)

 What did you conclude so far?

Please fill out the worksheet;

S. No.	Questions	Your Answers
1.	Why do school children face different types of psychological problems?	
2.	Who is responsible for causing problems in school children and why?	
3.	Do you think that the school in which you are studying gives you the "ideal" education? Why or why not?	
4.	From the list given above, what emotional-behavioral problems have you faced because of school?	
5.	Who is responsible for causing problems for you and why?	

S. No.	Questions	Your Answers
6.	What are your thinking patterns and decision-making styles behind your problems?	
7.	What are the factors that are or can aggravate your school-related problems?	
8.	How have your teachers/school system helped you to overcome your academic and other related emotional-behavioral problems?	
9.	How can your family help you to overcome your academic and other related emotional-behavioral problems?	
10.	What can you do by yourself to overcome your academic and other related emotional-behavioral problems?	

Psychologically speaking, school years are all about discoveries where you discover yourself, others, and the world through scaffolding done by the teachers. School and education at school should serve to be a forum where a child can practically go for discoveries and can identify, understand and unravel the mysteries of life. Presently, on a planet of 8.0 billion population, as that of November 2022, schools across the globe are catering to a diverse population of students. This multiculturalism is seen in terms of race, caste, religion, language, socio-economic status, and gender-ratio disparity. In the current era, there are inequalities in attaining education due to social stratification. Social stratification has brought many disparities with it, like; disparities in caste, religion, skin complexion, socio-economic status, and much more. These discrepancies are reflected in the school education system as a whole, particularly in the classroom. For example, in various countries, some students are more vulnerable as compared to others. Why? This is because of religious differences. In some schools, students of a particular religion are not allowed to enroll only because of religion-mismatch as the majority of the students, teachers, and administrators are of a different religion, while at other schools' students are harassed and victimized, again because of religious differences.

Schools across the sphere are developing and implementing different kinds of policies to minimize and eradicate these inequalities. For details, please go through the following;

- Nutrition levels of students are being enhanced to retain students, their attendance rates, and increase student enrolments.
- Access to education is being balanced for both boys and girls.
- Universalization of primary education is being emphasized.

- Education is being made accessible to the weaker sections of societies, including weaker castes and tribes.

- The marginalized population, disabled, and street children are also being targeted for school education.

- Financial aid and special incentives are being given to families who cannot afford school education for their children.

Despite all these efforts, school students experience a host of mild psychological problems to complex psychological disorders (as mentioned earlier). Along with the said, they experience biases, racism, discrimination, and stereotypical attitudes and behaviors from their classmates. Things get worse when the perpetrator is the teacher, the whole school system, and parents are unaware of the exact situation in which their child (or children) is/are being treated in school. Without a doubt, at this point, a child (a student) can go through intense emotional pain and suffering that could transform him/ her into a different personality – from an innocent being to a monster and from a discoverer to an ignorant and tunnel-minded personality.

At this point, the role of a teacher greatly matters as he/she is responsible for creating and maintaining a healthy classroom and learning environment. So, the characteristics and capabilities of a teacher play a significant role in understanding and building a sound personality and affecting the mental health of the students. Psychologically speaking, a teacher should ensure that instead of learning facts and figures about history, continent, country, culture, or the human body, students should learn to construct the concepts of any specific area, devise activities and abilities in that area which could be applied in practical life situations. In essence, good teachers understand and accept diversity among students not with reference to culture only but in terms of their different rates of development, set of different abilities that each student possesses, variations in language, and different home situations. Similarly, a teacher should adapt his/her teaching and assessment methodologies to that of the student's needs and capacities. Rather than moving solely through the course contents, the teacher should take care of the emotional needs of the pupils. All this should be the plan not only of the teachers but the entire school education system should take the responsibility to ensure an environment for the students that is nonjudgmental and non-discriminatory, and all students' self-esteem should be boosted. The environment should "enable" the students where they can learn to think rationally and apply this skill later in life, and they should not be limited only to reading and writing.

Activity Time (6.8)

Think of a teacher

Please fill out the worksheet;

S. No.	Questions	Your Answers
1.	What are the characteristics and qualities of your teacher that you love the most?	
2.	What are the characteristics of your teacher that you don't like at all?	
3.	Who is an "ideal" teacher, and why?	
4.	What makes you agree or disagree that a teacher is a role model?	
5.	For you, what makes an "ideal" classroom?	

What if you don't get a school, a teacher, a classroom, a company of students (classmates, juniors, and seniors), and a learning environment as per your needs, capacities, wishes, and desires? Of course, it will terribly affect you. It will affect your thoughts and emotional, physiological, and behavioral reactions, and if things are prolonged, this situation will intensely shake your mental health and overall personality. So, you need to keep an eye on the warning signs, which are actually indicators that your mental health is becoming affected by school, and when to take hold of yourself. The warning signs are enlisted below;

- ❗ Poor academic performance solely due to lack of motivation for school.

- ❗ Complete loss of interest in school work, including classwork and homework.

- ❗ Inability to experience joy and satisfaction in the classroom.

- ❗ Experiencing sadness and stress when it is something school-related.

- Preferring withdrawal and isolation over socializing and establishing relationships with other students.
- Feelings of tension and nervousness while going to school. In extreme cases, it can be triggered even by the thought of school.
- Butterflies in the stomach, nausea, and vomiting during assessment week or at the time of school, or in some cases, it can be triggered during school hours.
- Malingering to avoid school.
- Consistent, chronic, and unmanageable flashbacks of any school-related painful incident.
- Pervasive panic attacks, worry, and fearfulness related to attending or performing at school.
- Sleep difficulties include restless sleep and nightmares.
- Clearly refusing to attend school, preferring truancy, and/ or opting to drop out.
- A strong feeling of being rejected, discriminated and bullied on the basis of class, creed, or color.
- A strong feeling, wish or desire not to face the teacher.
- Anger outbursts due to any rational reason.

Test yourself

Please fill in the blanks with the very first word that pops up in your mind. Please DO NOT think. Write down the very first word that comes to your mind.

1. I wish to be a ___________________.

2. Currently, I am a _______________.

3. My school is __________________.

4. My teacher is ___________________.

5. My classroom is __________________.

6. My classmates are _________________.

7. My life in school is __________________.

8. My life after school is __________________.

9. My future is ________________.

10. My life is ___________________.

What did you notice about yourself through the game?

Please use the following to share your answer;

Things To Do

If you notice anything in yourself from the warning signs, then you need to do the following;

➡ Identify your thinking patterns about your school, teachers, classmates, and yourself (Details are discussed in chapter 3 of this book).

➡ Think and reflect on what you can practically do to come out of this unpleasant situation. (You may use the subsequent worksheets for this purpose). Will you try to change the situation, you're thinking patterns or your reactions? What can you do, and what will you do to bring a change and solve your existing problems?

➡ You may discuss your pain and suffering with your parents, a trustworthy friend, or an acquaintance. This way, you can generate a diverse pool of thinking patterns and coping strategies. It will be easy to choose and implement.

➡ Remember! Your things – psychological issues, pain, and agony is in your hands. So, you can either gather and make yourself or completely break yourself with your own hands. Please make it clear to yourself that nobody can better help you than "you."

➡ Think of a friend or an acquaintance or simply observe other students who are currently facing the same problems like those as yours. Identify their thinking patterns, decision-making styles, and coping mechanisms and try to adopt them.

➡ Try to think in a different way. Suppose your friend or a person you know very well is in the same situation and is thinking similarly to you. Their problems are similar to that you are currently struggling with. What advice/ suggestions would you give to him/her? How would you try to change his/her thoughts so that he/she can experience a change in the reactions (emotional, behavioral, and physiological)?

Use The Following Sheets To Help Yourself

Sheet 1

Ask yourself, "What's going through my head right now?" when you notice that your mood is deteriorating, write the thought or mental image down as soon as you can in the **Automatic Thought Column..**

DATE/ TIME	SITUATION	AUTOMATIC THOUGHT(S)	EMOTION(S)	ALTERNATIVE RESPONSE	OUTCOME
	1. What actual event or stream of thoughts, daydreams, or recollection led to the unpleasant emotion? 2. What (if any) distressing physical sensations did you have?	1. What thought(s) and/ or image(s) went through your mind? 2. How much did you believe each one at the time?	1. What emotion(s) (sad, anxious, angry, etc.) did you feel at the time? 2. How intense (0-100%) was the emotion?	1. Use the questions at the bottom to compose a response to the automatic thought(s). 2. How much do you believe in each response?	1. How much do you now believe in each automatic thought? 2. What emotion(s) do you feel now? How intense (0-100%) is the emotion?

Questions to help compose an alternative response:

- What is the evidence that the automatic thought is true? Not true?

- Is there an alternative explanation?

- What's the worst that could happen, and how could you cope? What's the best that could happen? What's the most realistic outcome?

- What's the effect of believing the automatic thought? What could be the effect of changing my thinking?

- If _____________ (friend's name) were in the situation, what would I tell him/her? What would I do about it?

Sheet 2

Sometimes you may find yourself completely drowned in negative automatic thoughts like stressing about an upcoming exam. You may think something like, "Okay, I am not prepared for the exam, but since I am good at English and because I have done some reading, I can perform." Similarly, you may think, "My friend Nick is good at school, he/she thinks like this and this, and I can think in that way too."

Give it a try now. In the left column, write down negative thoughts, and in the right column, jot down positive facts which are there around a problem, and you can turn it into your strengths and opportunities to rise and succeed.

S. No.	Negative Thoughts/ Problematic Thoughts/ Painful Thoughts/ Unwanted Thoughts	Possible Positive Facts (What can I do in the face of adversity?)

Sheet 3

Jot down your negative thoughts in the left column and invest some time in suggesting solutions at the thinking and/or behavioral level or simply suggest alternative paths (solutions) strong enough to smoothly navigate you through your problems. For example, John might think that the teacher is biased and stereotypical toward him. This thought could be true, but what can he do to overcome his problem? He can talk to the teacher privately for clarification; he can be assertive in expressing his thoughts and feelings. He could join a group of good classmates and make friends to feel secure and more confident etc.

Now try for yourself:

S. No.	Negative Thoughts	Possible Changes in Thinking/ Behavior or Alternatives To Solve a Problem

I am The World

Search and briefly learn about the following painful incidents and attempt activity 7.1. This will allow you to understand the current chapter in a better way;

- ⌖ Christchurch Mosque Shootings (2019)
- ⌖ Halle synagogue Shootings (2019)
- ⌖ Sri Lanka Easter Bombings (2019)
- ⌖ Jolo Cathedral Bombings (2019)
- ⌖ Hanau Shootings (2020)
- ⌖ Vienna Attack (2020)
- ⌖ Dar es Salaam Shooting (2021)
- ⌖ London, Ontario Truck Attack (2021)
- ⌖ Buffalo Shooting (2022)
- ⌖ Colorado Springs nightclub shooting (2022)

What did you search about the thinking styles/ patterns of the perpetrators?

Please use the following to share your answer;

Police and other security forces, journalists, and newscasters talk about the role of extremism, far-right extremism, religious extremism, terrorism, antisemitism, racism, and prejudice against religion behind all the massacres stated above. All of them ignore the formation and impact of "core beliefs."

In order to fully understand core beliefs, you need to understand beliefs.

Beliefs begin to form from early childhood. The age and stage cannot be specified as mental health professionals around the globe conclude that when an infant starts to understand and make sense of his surroundings and environment, certain beliefs begin to form. The beliefs are broadly divided into three categories;

- About one's self
- About others
- About the world

The role of caregivers, family members, education, community, and mass media in the formation of beliefs has been greatly emphasized by social scientists and mental health professionals worldwide. An infant at the stage of crawling observes and concludes. For example, my father is there to grab me and play with me. He/ she, therefore, will smile or giggle at the sight of the father because the infant has formed a positive, constructive belief about the father. Of course, these beliefs are not articulated by the infants, but they are well understood by their emotional display and the ways they react and behave in the presence and absence of others. On the contrary, a toddler is severely reprimanded by his/ her father for playing with a ball or for jumping in the presence of guests. As a consequence, a toddler may form a negative, destructive belief about the father. Severe and harsh incidents and repeated negative, painful, and destructive experiences of the infants yield to negative, poor, and destructive beliefs about the self, others, and the world. On the other side, if the experiences of the children are healthy and positive, undoubtedly, it will yield a positive, constructive, and strong set of beliefs about the self, others, and the world. It is hypothesized that, most probably, in the former scenario, the individual would be filled with disgust, hate, and revenge. In the latter case, the individual would be peaceful, loving, caring, and forgiving. Yes, it is the power of the beliefs which are formed from childhood.

Look at your beliefs.

Please fill in the blanks with the very first word that pops up in your mind. Please DO NOT think. Write down the very first word that comes to your mind.

1. I am a ____________________.

2. Others are ____________________.

3. The world is ____________________.

4. I think I am a ____________________.

5. I think others are ____________________.

6. I think the world is ____________________.

7.   I wish others could be ___________________.

8.   I wish I could be a ___________________.

9.   I wish the world would be a ___________________.

10.   People are ___________________.

11.   I want to ___________________.

12.   Others want to ___________________.

13.   The world wants to ___________________.

14.   Others see me as a ___________________.

15.   My future is ___________________.

Core beliefs are central. It is a set of beliefs that are enduring understandings so fundamental and deep that they often are not articulated. They are the "silent" beliefs that are operational, acting as your "drivers" and serve to be a navigator of your reactions, emotional, physiological, and behavioral. Thus, core beliefs are not articulated to oneself and are taken as "absolute truths."

Explain or simply jot down some of your core beliefs or "absolute truths."

Please use the following to share your answer;

Core beliefs are the most fundamental level of belief; they are global, rigid, and overgeneralized. The individual carries these beliefs with him/ her, and they get or can easily be activated in any situation, and the reactions are affected. By now, I assume that you have learned the concept of automatic thoughts. Automatic thoughts are the real words and/ or images that go through an individual's mind. As you have learned, they are beyond one's voluntary control. They pop up in the blink of an eye or like a flashlight. For a better understanding of the relationship between core beliefs and automatic thoughts, kindly go through the following;

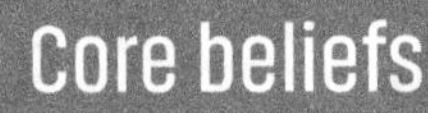

Core beliefs lead to Automatic thoughts

It is exactly like the following;

Genotype (genetic composition) leads to Phenotype (observable characteristics)

In Cognitive Behavioral Therapy (CBT), it is believed that there is a hypothetical container somewhere inside the mind of the entire mankind where core beliefs are formed and stored. For better clarification, have a look at the following;

Core beliefs are of different themes. For details and better clarification, kindly go through the following list of core beliefs;

Helpless core beliefs	Unlovable core beliefs	Worthless core beliefs
I am incompetent	I am unlovable	I am worthless
I am ineffective	I am unlikeable	I am unacceptable
I can't do anything right	I am undesirable	I am bad
I am helpless	I am unattractive	I am a waste
I am powerless	I am unwanted	I am immoral
I am weak	I am uncared for	I am dangerous
I am vulnerable	I am different	I am toxic
I am a victim	I am bad, so others will not love me	I am evil
I am needy	I am defective so others will not love me	I don't deserve to live
I am a failure	I am bound to be rejected	I am unpleasant

Do you believe you have a core belief(s) from the list above?

From the above list, choose the core beliefs that you think you possess. Explain the "why" as well. What factors were/are responsible for its formation and sustenance?

Please use the following to share your answer;

In the case of no, highlight the factors you think are responsible for the absence of the core beliefs.

Please use the following to share your answer;

No matter what kind of core belief is carried by an individual, it is formed through the environment and is maintained/ reinforced by the environment. Kindly go through the following illustration;

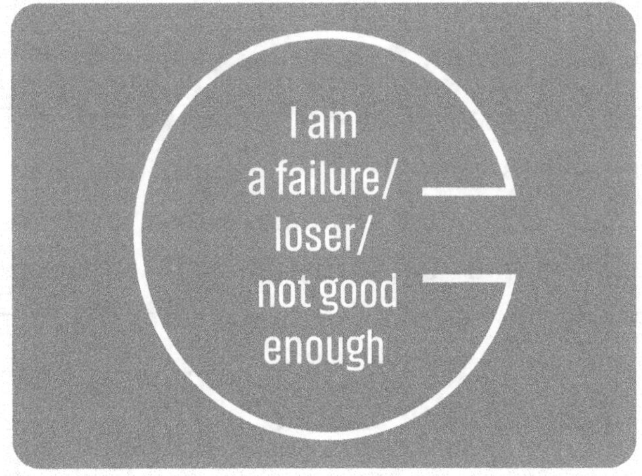

This picture shows a schema consisting of core beliefs;

- 🔁 "I am a failure."
- 🔁 "I am a loser."
- 🔁 "I am not good enough."

Let's see how core beliefs are strengthened through the environment;

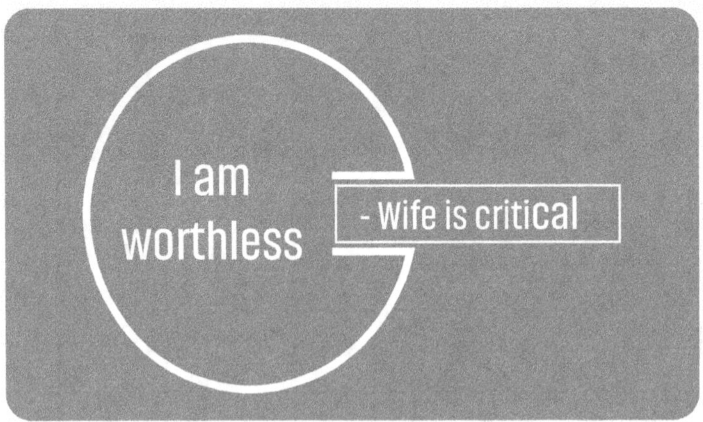

Nathan, a 27-year-old married male, has the core belief "I am worthless." As mentioned earlier, a core belief is an "absolute truth." So, for Nathan, regardless of the reality or evidence to the contrary, his core belief is 100% true. This "degree of belief" in the core belief will change Nathan's broad (general) views to narrow views, and thus he will become tunnel-minded or tunnel-focused. Whether his wife is critical of him or not, he will put those comments inside the schema, and therefore his core belief will always be, "I am worthless." Of course, Nathan's wife would be appreciative at times, but it would be most likely that Nathan would ignore this as his primary focus would only be on the aspects that are capable enough to reinforce and strengthen his core belief. A hypothetical mechanism has been explained via the illustration above.

Strengthening/ reinforcing your core belief(s).

How would you strengthen/ reinforce your core belief(s)? What happens in the environment? What comments did you put in your schema to reinforce your core beliefs?

Please use the following to share your answer;

Now let's talk about intermediate beliefs. Intermediate beliefs are rules, attitudes, and assumptions that exist between core beliefs and automatic thoughts. Let's see the following picture;

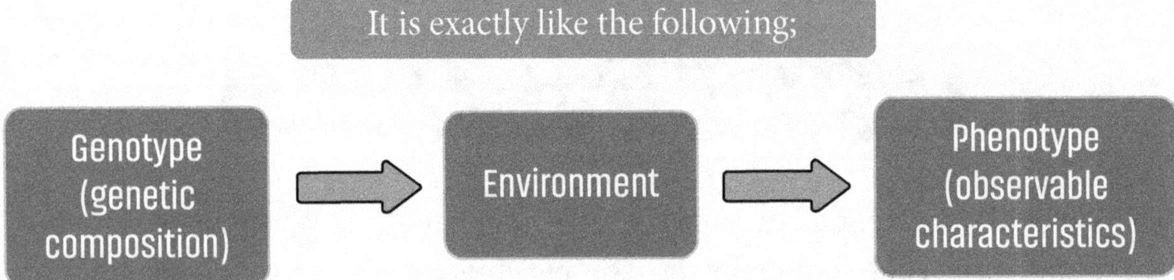

People try to make sense of their environment from their early developmental stages. They need to organize their experience in a coherent way in order to function adaptively. Their interactions with the world and other people, influenced by their genetic predisposition, lead to certain understandings: their beliefs (all kinds of beliefs), which may vary in their accuracy and functionality. Cognitive Behavioral Therapy (CBT) helps to unlearn negative, disastrous, and "dysfunctional" beliefs, and reality-based, functional, and "constructive" new beliefs are formed and strengthened. The most instant and effective way to help others feel better and behave more adaptively is to facilitate the direct modification of their core beliefs as soon as possible. This exercise will help an individual to interpret future situations or problems in a more practical way.

Examples of core beliefs, intermediate beliefs, and automatic thoughts

Hypothetical Scenario:

Yesenia, a 10-year-old Hispanic girl, most of the time she has been seen sad in her mathematics class for the last six months, and upon being asked by the teacher, she reported that she wants to get rid of mathematics class and that she is not at all interested in the subject. Yesenia also added that she feels palpitations and sweating during her classes of mathematics.

As per our learning from the previous chapters of this book, firstly, we should identify all reactions of Yesenia;

⮕ Sadness is Yesenia's emotional reaction.

⮕ Palpitations and sweating are Yesenia's physiological reactions.

⮕ Getting rid of or avoiding mathematics class is Yesenia's behavioral reaction.

Yesenia's core beliefs, intermediate beliefs, and automatic thoughts are unknown so far. *So, let's try to solve the riddle together.*

Yesenia's <u>automatic thoughts</u> could be something like;

- 💬 "I am unable to do mathematics class,"
- 💬 "I am not able to perform well in math class,"
- 💬 "I am not made for this particular subject,"
- 💬 "Mathematics is boring,"
- 💬 "The teacher is not suitable for mathematics."

Yesenia's <u>intermediate beliefs</u> (rules, attitudes, and assumptions) could be something like this;

- 💬 "I should give up" (rule),
- 💬 "I will fail in mathematics" (assumption),
- 💬 "It would be terrible to fail" (attitude),
- 💬 "I am not made for this horrible subject" (rule and attitude),
- 💬 "Mathematics is boring" (attitude),

Yesenia's <u>core belief</u> could be something like the following;

- 💬 "I am incompetent."

Do Yesenia's core beliefs, intermediate beliefs, and automatic thoughts make sense to you? Most probably, this cognitive framework is activated before and/ or during mathematics class, which of course, is the "situation" component in the basic cognitive model. Yesenia's beliefs and reactions stem from her core belief, and she most probably is narrowing her focus consistently when she is attending to those stimuli and pieces of information which are confirming her core belief. That is why she experienced negative and destructive emotional, physiological and behavioral reactions.

Activity Time (7.5)

Help Yesenia

By now, you must be well aware of Yesenia's cognitive functioning and perceptions. So, how can you help her to come out of this?

Please use the following to share your answer;

Only after successfully learning and applying all the concepts that have been elaborated in this book so far can you work, identify and change your core beliefs.

Alabama has the core belief, "I am a loser." He looks and processes information from his environment in such a manner that he just strengthens his core belief, and he involuntarily ignores and discards the contradicting (or mismatching) information to that of the core belief. This core belief triggers when Alabama is not able to understand any complex topic in history class.

Let's give Alabama a worksheet like the following;

Name: Alabama

Old Core Belief: "I am a loser."

New Core Belief: Like everybody else, I possess certain strengths and weaknesses.

Let's encourage Alabama to work on his new core belief. He should identify all the factors, efforts, and present and past achievements to support the new core belief. Alabama's responses should be something like the following;

Evidence that contradicts the old core belief and supports the new belief	Evidence that seems to support the old core belief with reframe
I understand complex topics in English class.	I don't understand History related content very well, but after doing some homework, I feel more comfortable. This can happen to anybody.
I am a punctual and regular student; I have never missed a history class. If I was a loser, I would have avoided history class.	I admit that I am disinterested and weak in History class. This could be because I don't practice it like other subjects.

Work on your core beliefs.

Evidence that contradicts an old core belief and supports a new belief	Evidence that seems to support an old core belief with reframe

Now help Yesenia to work on her core beliefs.

Evidence that contradicts an old core belief and supports a new belief	Evidence that seems to support an old core belief with reframe

All painful incidents, like harming oneself and others, killing other people, etc., are because of core beliefs, as mentioned, which are formed and strengthened as a result of repeated experiences and interactions with the environment, parents, teachers, the mass media, etc. Therefore, reactions end up with discrimination, racism, prejudice, and even terrorism. Technically what is happening inside the mind is deeper beliefs: rules, attitudes, and assumptions are being set on this "destructive" theme, and therefore they work on this pattern. In an opposite situation, an individual can have pleasurable/positive core beliefs such as "I am honest," "I am brave," and "I am helpful," which will positively affect his intermediate beliefs (rules, attitudes, and assumptions) and an individual would be peaceful, constructive and productive in his life. He/ she would be noble, generous, and a lifesaver to others.

By keeping this all-in view, it can be concluded that each one of us carries an independent world that comes from our core beliefs. Due to this, we can either be fruitful and constructive in our daily life or be unproductive and miserable. Thus, "I am the world" becomes a proven fact.

Cognitive Discipline

Carefully go through the following;

➡ Work on automatic thoughts before modifying beliefs.

➡ Teach to disciple yourself to first learn to identify automatic thoughts that connect to the deeper-level beliefs. Failing to see the larger picture, you will be less likely to work on the beliefs.

➡ Learn to identify and reframe negative automatic thoughts before going to intermediate beliefs and core beliefs. You will do it by noticing a change or a shift in your mood and emotions.

☞ From mood and emotions move to automatic thoughts, then beliefs: intermediate beliefs and core beliefs.

☞ Remember, there is no mega change, a grand activity, a grand, or a perfect solution to change thinking patterns. The solution comes from daily life commitment and consistency, where you work on your cognitions.

☞ Go through chapter 4 of this book, and revise the concept of "cortical" evolution. Yes, the brain is unique and miraculous.

This worksheet can be used to identify automatic thoughts and to help you come up with alternative thoughts.

➡ What is the situation?

➡ What am I thinking or imagining?

➡ How does that make me feel?   mad   sad   nervous

other:

➡ What makes me think the thought is true?

➡ What makes me think the thought is not true or partially true?

➡ What can be another way to look at this particular situation?

➡ What could happen if I changed my thinking?

➡ What would I tell my friend [think of a specific person] if this happened to him or her?

➡ What can be my final decision now?

This worksheet can be used to identify core beliefs, intermediate beliefs (rules, attitudes, and assumptions), and automatic thoughts and reactions: emotional, physiological, and behavioral.

➮ My core belief(s):

➮ My intermediate beliefs:

➮ My automatic thoughts:

➮ My reactions: Emotional:

Behavioral:

Physiological:

This set of questions can help you to identify the "words" of your automatic thoughts in a situation. The discovery can help you to connect with deeper beliefs.

1. What was/ is going through my mind?

2. What am I/ was I thinking?

3. Was I anticipating/expecting anything?

4. What was I predicting would happen?

5. What did I think about my ability to handle/cope with this situation?

This worksheet can help you to identify the "costs" and "benefits" of believing in your automatic thoughts, particularly "core beliefs." The discovery can help you either to distance yourself from believing in your current beliefs or to change them.

(Please use one sheet per core belief and/or automatic thought. DO NOT hesitate to expand the lists. You will discover more by writing more.)

Current core belief: OR   Current automatic thought:

Benefits/ advantages of holding on to this core belief and/ or automatic thought	Costs/ disadvantages of holding on to this core belief and/ or automatic thought

This worksheet can help you to understand the "thought-response" connection. You think, and you respond. The other way around, the way you think affects the way you respond.

THOUGHTS (I THINK . . . . .)	RESPONSES (THEREFORE, I RESPOND . . . . .)
<u>Example:</u> I think I can be a doctor.	<u>Example:</u> I will most likely be talking more about body parts, organs, diseases, and medicine because I "think" I can be a doctor.

This worksheet can help you to identify and understand the "dirty tricks" that your mind plays with you. In the left-hand column, write your automatic thoughts, and in the right-hand column, write down the dirty tricks.

(Revise chapter 4 for better understanding)

AUTOMATIC THOUGHTS	DIRTY TRICKS
Example: Joseph thinks and feels that all girls are shy.	Example: Robert (Joseph's friend) asks why he thinks that way. Joseph tells Robert that this is due to his gut feelings only. This is a dirty trick known as 'prisoner of feeling.'

This is the advanced worksheet of worksheet #7. It can help you to generate a more rational, factual, and logical way of viewing things.

AUTOMATIC THOUGHTS	DIRTY TRICKS

1. What would be a more rational, factual, or logical way to view things?

2. How would I feel if I thought differently about all the mentioned things?

This worksheet can help you to "identify" and "examine" the evidence of your automatic thought(s). In the left-hand column, jot down the supporting pieces of evidence, and in the right-hand column, enlist the pieces of evidence which are against the automatic thought(s).

Current automatic thought:

Evidence "for" the automatic thought (Supporting evidence)	Evidence "against" the automatic thought (Evidence to the contrary)

This worksheet can help you to "identify" situations, automatic thoughts, and reactions (emotional, behavioral, and physiological).

(Go through chapter # 2 for more details)

Situation	AUTOMATIC THOUGHTS	Reactions

LIFE SKILLS

Today, mankind is facing a lot of problems, such as global warming, famines, poverty, and population explosion. In addition to this, there are different kinds of psychological problems from which suicide is escalating. If you look around, there is "endless" competition, or what mental health professionals like to call "cut-throat" competition, visible in all walks of life. Similarly, We often witness people around us worried about their jobs because there is a lack of job security. Another group of people is finding it difficult to find employment. They have to go through a lot of pain to successfully land a job as unemployment is one of the emerging global issues that is originating from a high rate of population growth.

In this global scenario, clinicians, social scientists, academicians, and professionals belonging to other disciplines focus on young minds. For all the experts and dignitaries, youngsters are considered the most productive members of society due to their physical and intellectual capabilities. But what is happening in reality? Are these young minds really capable enough to cope with the emerging global challenges? Why or why not?

Have you ever observed yourself as a youngster or other youngsters around you who are unable to utilize their potential in constructive and productive ways? What are some of the reasons you think are holding young minds back from utilizing their physical and mental capabilities?

Please use the following to share your answer;

A group of mental health professionals concludes that it is due to a lack of guidance and motivation. Another group of professionals comes to a conclusion by highlighting social problems such as smoking, chemical addiction, sexual abuse, juvenile delinquency, anti-social acts, etc. All such problems have an adverse effect on young brains and others, too, when talking about the larger picture.

Let's discuss what you can do to ensure you achieve your full potential.

Bringing Life Skills in "Life"

Life skills are a range of psychosocial and cognitive abilities that equip an individual to make informed decisions, generate multiple and alternate options, understand and manage one's own emotions to maintain emotional well-being, and communicate effectively with others. All this helps an individual to deal effectively with the demands and challenges of everyday life.
There is a need to develop scholastic as well as co-scholastic areas among young children throughout the planet. There is a mutual consensus among educationists, theorists, and clinicians that life skills bridge the gap between basic functioning and capabilities. It strengthens the ability of children to meet emerging issues and problems. Thus, a relevant life skills education helps in dealing with the current global issues in such a manner that is practical.

Life skills are a behavior development approach designed to address the balance of the following areas:

➡ Knowledge

➡ Attitude

➡ Skills

There are ten core life skills which are as follows;

1. Self-awareness
2. Critical thinking
3. Creative thinking
4. Decision making
5. Problem Solving
6. Effective communication
7. Interpersonal relationship
8. Empathy
9. Coping with stress
10. Coping with emotion

Life skills have been classified into three broad categories:

S. No.	Life Skills	Description
1.	Thinking skills	Thinking skills enhance the "logic" side of your brain. This is done by using analytical abilities, creative thinking, and creative abilities, developing problem-solving skills, and through improving decision-making abilities.
2.	Social skills	This set of skills includes interpersonal skills, communication skills, leadership skills, and management skills.
3.	Emotional skills	Emotional skills refer to the knowledge and abilities to know about "the self" and are comfortable with it. It is the self-management or protection of "the self" from family and peer pressures. Thus, it is all about managing/ coping with the given circumstances.

From the above, which life skill do you think you possess the most? What factors make you better at it?

OR

What makes you think that you don't possess these life skills?

Please use the following to share your answer;

Functions of Life Skills

The functions of life skills are as follows;

- ➡ It enhances critical thinking.
- ➡ It fosters a sense of responsibility and future planning.
- ➡ It improves physical and psychological well-being.
- ➡ Cooperative/ collaborative and prosocial behaviors are increased.
- ➡ Life skills reduce chemical addiction, problems related to self-confidence and self-esteem, self-destructive behaviors, and aggression.
- ➡ It boosts social and emotional adjustment. Thus, there is better tolerance and adjustment with diverse people.

How to Learn Life Skills

You will be surprised to know that by incorporating simple activities into your daily life, you can learn and enhance your life skills. It can be done through sports, drama, or storytelling. You can find some ways in the below section:

Discussions:

In discussions, you speak your ideas to others and, in return, listen to the views, opinions, and ideas of others. Instead of a monologue, discussions consist of dialogue. Therefore, discussions allow you the opportunity to deepen your understanding of the subject matter, and undoubtedly you can develop skills like listening, empathy and assertiveness.

Brainstorming:

By sitting in a group and getting imaginative, will get you to think outside the box. This will eventually allow you to generate a pool of ideas that you will be able to rank according to criteria. After thorough practice, you will be able to generate ideas instantly, as brainstorming enhances thinking and social skills.

Storytelling:

Storytelling directly enhances critical thinking. Critical thinking, as a final outcome, leads to drawing certain metaphors and/ or analogies and constructive solutions. In addition to it, storytelling strengthens listening, attention, patience and endurance. So, you should definitely read or listen to different stories from different cultures.

Debates:

Debates affect your creativity and in-depth analysis about a particular topic, for example, "Education for all," "Importance of technology," "Public health," and much more. Debates will allow you to state and defend your views and perspectives; thus, it brings an opportunity for you to work on higher-order thinking like planning, reasoning, and logic.

Activity Time (8.3)

From the above, which method(s) will you practice in order to enhance your life skills and why?

Please use the following to share your answer;

Life skills are the need of the hour under current circumstances. It gives youngsters a set of skills for life adjustments. The skills are practical and strengthen cognitive, psychological, and self-management skills. Life skills, therefore, are psychosocial interventions to improve the mental health of our youngsters by lifting their critical thinking, problem-solving, decision-making, and coping strategies and boosting their self-confidence and self-esteem. Practitioners, theorists, and researchers claim that life skills education should be part of the curriculum, and teachers should be trained enough to impart it to their students. Similarly, parents should assimilate certain ways and methods in their parenting that should bring life skills education into their children's life for the betterment of their children in every way. It is worth mentioning that cognitive behavioral therapy (CBT) and life skills move together. CBT is like the cleansing of thoughts and the way we make sense of this world and life skills to move around the world, cope, and dominate emerging problems and complex challenges. Thus, both should be considered together.

My final request...

Being a smaller author, reviews help me out tremendously!

It would mean a lot to me if you could leave a review.

If you enjoyed this workbook and learned a thing or two, please let me know!

It only takes 30 seconds but means so much to me!

CONCLUSION

So, how do you feel after going through this workbook? Are you feeling more self-assured, confident, centered, happy, and resilient? As a human, it is important that you first examine your default settings (biological factors) and learn and/ or influence agents from the environment (psychosocial factors). Later, understand the inclinations that you express through words, symbols, emotions, desires, and certain sets of behaviors so that you may later be able to see where change is needed. Taking some time to see yourself in a mirror would work a little, but taking some time to see yourself, your future, others, and the world with different glasses and a new perspective would be the first step toward a powerful change.

Identifying and understanding automatic thoughts to eventually identify, understand, and "change" deeper beliefs would promptly lead you to the stage of self-actualization, where you can cultivate a lot in your own backyard. Remember, background noise will crowd your thoughts. It is normal and natural. It happens with everybody, but success is in scheduling your daily life routine. It is mandatory for you to allocate some time for yourself where it is only you and your thoughts. There is no grand solution for any of your difficulties and problems. Results come from daily life commitment and dedication to practicing and applying the activities given in this book. Each of you is on a life path that ought to be constructed by your choices, paved with your experiences, and aimed in the direction of your dreams. You should not allow anybody to take this privilege from you. Build your self-efficacy by taking control of yourself and taking responsibility for your cognitive functioning. Through this set of skills, show to the world that the choices you make, the decisions you take, and the principles you value not only carry short-term gains but will lead you to a fulfilling adult life.

Resources

- Beck, J. S. (2011). *Cognitive behavior therapy: Basics and beyond* (2nd ed.). Guilford Press.

- Leahy, R. L. (2017). *Cognitive Therapy Techniques: A Practitioner's Guide.* (2nd Ed.): New York, NY: Guilford Press

- United Nations Department of Economic and Social Affairs, Population Division (2022). World

- Population Prospects 2022: Summary of Results. UN DESA/POP/2022/TR/NO. 3

- https://courses.lumenlearning.com/wm-introductiontosociology/chapter/defining-family/#:~:text=Family%20is%20a%20socially,how%20one%20enters%20into%20them